RIDDLE AND REVERIE

THE MACMILLAN COMPANY
NEW YORK · BOSTON · CHICAGO · DALLAS
ATLANTA · SAN FRANCISCO

MACMILLAN & CO., Limited
LONDON · BOMBAY · CALCUTTA
MELBOURNE

THE MACMILLAN COMPANY
OF CANADA, Limited
TORONTO

RIDDLE AND REVERIE

BY

Leonard Feeney, S. J.

NEW YORK
THE MACMILLAN COMPANY
1933

TO

MY FATHER

The author is grateful to the Editor of *America* for permission to reprint: *Mouse Trap, Sara Finn* and *Grandmother Lou;* and to the Editor of the *Saturday Review of Literature* for permission to reprint *The Organ Blower.*

CONTENTS

RIDDLE AND REVERIE

THE GOLD I HAVE GATHERED

The gold I have gathered I mined in my mind,
The beautiful beauty God helped me to find.

The wonderful wonder I hoard in my head,
I said I will share it with someone; I said

I will put in a poem an inkling in ink
Of the love that I live by, the truth that I think.

And the wealth of my wisdom I thought I could tell,
My hunger for Heaven, my horror of Hell,

With some poor little scribbles I make with a pen.
Now fancy THAT, ladies and gentlemen!

THE DOVE

Learn from a little dove,
  The Holy Spirit's symbol,
The qualities of love,
  And what it must resemble.

Notice its note will vary
  At different seasons,—
A wild bird, and a wary,
  For different reasons.

When sunlight warms the roof,
  And moonlight fills the nest,
Innocent, soft, aloof,
  Unruffled and at rest.

But when the storm is raging:
  Clawing, battling, crying;
A bird beyond all caging,
  Furiously flying.

I BURNED MY BRIDGES

I burned my bridges when I had crossed.
I never brooded on what I lost,
Nor ruined with rapine my holocaust.

Youth is a rapture we must forget;
Wither and wrinkle without regret,
Hobble to Heaven and do not fret.

Yet in my soul there is something still
Deeper than memory, mind and will,
Something alive that I cannot kill.

Part of me, put not in my keeping,
Awakes unwakened when I am sleeping,
Under my laughter it goes on weeping

For bye-gone beaches and limbs of brown,
When hoops were rolling around the town,
And London Bridges were falling down.

THE GIFT OF TEARS

Never a rhyme I wrote or read
    Could ever make me cry;
But a little brown fiddle
Sawed in the middle
    Does, and I don't know why.

SPRING CAROL

My little joy, my sweet joy,
   I wish I could romance it;
I wish I had a light foot
   Deft enough to dance it,
   Or pictures to portray it,
   Or syllables to say it,
Or wind enough to fill a flute
   And play it.

REFLECTION

When we were young and you were fond
Of rolling pebbles in a pond,
Remember how we waded out
And looked and found without a doubt
Our pictures near a silver school
Of little fishes in a pool?

Though round the world the rivers go
And into fussy fountains flow,
Our pictures shall remain
When waters rest again.
The mirror in the well will not
Forget us when we are forgot.

SMALL FRY

I went fishing for a rhyme
   In the babble of a brook
And a merry little minnow
   Nibbled at my hook,
And here's the pretty fellow
   Bouncing in a book.

MY WINDOW

I lock my window tight,
I bolt it with a bar,
Ever since the night
One memorable star
Came shining through,
And made unusually bright
My parallelogram of light,
My acre in the blue.
I cover my window too
With a dark curtain
So to be certain
No one else will try
To trespass with his eye
On my part of the sky.

BRIEF LITANY

Softly out of nowhere
  Blows a summer breeze,
Wrinkling in the sunshine,
  Trembling in the trees;

Swings a little trinket
  Hanging in the air,
Keeps a penny pin-wheel
  Twirling at a fair;

Starts a wee melodeon
  Pumping in a flea,
Stops and drops a lobster
  A bubble in the sea;

Turns into a tremolo,
  Flows through a fife;
Lends a tiny hop-toad
  A lungful of life;

Falters on the hill-top,
  Tumbles down the glen,
Buried in a world
  Without wind. Amen.

SHEEP RITUAL

Oh you should have seen the miracle
  I saw when I was in Wales,
Where myriads of sheep go munching up
  And lunching down the dales;
And graze along the meadow marsh,
  And nibble around the mill,
Cross the bridges over the brook,
  Bleat and eat and fill
Their bellies full of blossoms;
  Then lie awhile and sleep.
Then slowly up the slope again
  And slowly down the steep,
Their little mouths meandering on,
  Bite by bite they pull,
Inch by inch, the sweet grass
  While all the beautiful
Valleys of Wye from stream to sky
  Are turning into wool.

AT THE FIREPLACE

The mulberry logs are covered with flame
  And lacquered with light they burn.
The trick of the blazing mulberry logs
  In the grate, is my great concern:—

How all this essence of fiery juice
  And fibre and gnarl and knot
Is now transmuted to whistle and multiple
  Crackle and pistol shot.

The mulberry logs, so stiff and tough,
  Substantial and hard and round,
Astound me, vanishing—save for an ounce
  Of ash—into so much sound.

JOY IN HEAVEN

Jesus clapped His little hands
   And Mary lit a star
When I helped an old lady with bundles
   Onto a trolley car.

MOUSE TRAP

I never kill a caught mouse
  Nor drown him in a pail.
I always extricate him
  And lift him by the tail,

And carefully release him
  Into the hollow wall,
Because I do admire a mouse
  Who is not sceptical;

Who keeps his faith in odors
  That terminate in cheese,
And will not rob his little nose
  Of all its certainties.

I loathe an apprehensive mouse
  Whose phobia for traps
Reduces life's philosophy
  To "maybe" and "perhaps";

Who holds that truth is relative,
  Who disbelieves in smell,
And spreads despair in micedom
  And turns it into Hell.

Give me a trustful little mouse
  Who chisels in and out
And grinds his way to surety
  And chews away a doubt,

And turns my house to splinters
   To satisfy his soul,
And breaks his gallant little neck
   Exploring in a hole.

MOTH MEMORIES

God's baby dew-moth dancing down the dawn,
Flitting from leaf to leaf along the lawn,
Squanders its dainty substance in the air
And leaves no sweet remembrance anywhere,

Save in some moody lady's elegies
Concerning moths, mosquitoes, flies and fleas,
Who pouts in poems, like an owl or pigeon,
Her whit-tu-whu and jug-a-jug religion.

THE FIRST DAY OF CREATION

When God tried out His thunderbolts
  And lightnings wildly lightened,
It frightens me to think there was
  Nobody to be frightened.

PROBLEM

The white invisible angels
  We clothe in queer disguises,
In wings and snowy night-gowns
  To suit our strange surmises.

But how do they see in symbols
  Of unethereal air
Old Pudgy, our parish fat man,
  Puffing his little prayer?

THE STREET SPRINKLERS

When whistling teamsters down the hills
  Their bubbling barrels drive again,
Scattering liquid whippoorwills
And thrushes from a rolling brush,
  Our ears become alive again
  Listening to the luscious noises.
Hosannas from the hoses rush
  And all the air rejoices.

POOR TURKEY

The melancholy turkey-cock,
Of every bird the laughing stock,
Stands bewildered beside the barn,
Endeavoring to gobble a yard of yarn;
And folds his foliage like a fan,
And pecks at popcorn in a pan;
And wobbles and winks and wonders why
For all his feathers he cannot fly,
Hysterically hiccuping
A little song he cannot sing.

PRAY FOR ME

Pray for me when I was small,
   When I was two or three,
The night when nobody at all
   Prayed for me;

When nobody knew they left me out
   And lost me in the snow.
God help me when I tried to shout,
   Long ago.

INEVITABLE RENDEZVOUS

Down at Oyster Graveyard
  Sitting on a quay,
One afternoon in April
  From three till half past three,
I felt so much emotion
I got the silly notion
That God made the ocean
  From all eternity
  Exclusively for me.
And I'd like to know exactly
  Did He or didn't He?

SIMPLIFICATION

Lucky for girls nimble with thimbles
    Poems and plays are lies.
Love is as simple and sane as sewing,
    A problem of hooks and eyes.

He had a hole in his Sunday stocking,
    She with her needle mended it:—
That was the wonder of wife and woman,
    That was the trick that ended it.

Lucky for dreamy organ grinders
    And strolling umbrella menders;
Lucky for lonely deep-sea divers
    And telephone-pole ascenders.

THE PIANO TUNER

Do, re, *moo!*
Do, re, *meow!*
  Sounds so far
  Like a cat or a cow.

Do, re, *miff!*
Do, re, *muff!*
  Guess I haven't
  It tight enough.

Do, re, *measles!*
Do, re, *mumps!*
  Turn it too tight
  And back it jumps.

Do, re, (listen!)
Do, re, *MI!*
  There's the little bird
  I heard in a tree!

BLIND MAN'S POEM

I've snapped all my fingers
   And scratched all my hair.
I'm tired of being someplace
   Sitting in a chair.
I think I shall get up now
   And go to anywhere.

THE PRISONER

Monday I whistled a little.
 Tuesday I whistled a lot.

Wednesday I whistled a little.
 Thursday I have forgot.

Friday I whistled a little.
 But not on Saturday.

Sunday I whistled a little;
 The jailer came in to say:

"Hello", and I whistled a little
 After he went away.

"Therefore the transition from a coloured shape to the notion of an object which can be used for all sorts of purposes which have nothing to do with colour, seems a very natural one and we . . . require careful training if we are to refrain from acting upon it."

PROFESSOR PUFFLES.

Giddily in the garden
  The little bee blows,
With wax on his waistcoat
  And treacle on his toes,
  And a noise in his nose;
Pausing at a pansy
  And reposing on a rose.

Gee! but it must be jolly
  For a bee to be a bee,
And to jab a juicy javelin
  In a nice anemone
  That has objectivity,
As arranged by Aristotle
  In his strange philosophy.

Merrily in the meadow
  This fuzzy fellow fills
His engine full of honey
  On the sunny petal-sills
  Of delicious daffodils,
With an illative indifference
  To his inferential ills.

Really it must be rapture
    To buzz about the brink
Of a violet that is valid
    Or an *a priori* pink,
    Even though one's color kink
Is the fruit of careless training
    In thinking how to think.

FERVERINO IN A FRUIT STORE

Out of nothing God made each,
Made a poet, and made a peach.
God His nothings could confound,
Out of nothings switched around,
Make a bard
Green and hard;
Make a mellow
Fruit a fellow.
Neither would have known.
One would bother
With a rhyme,
And eat the other
Every time.
Skin and bone,
Or skin and stone:—
Praised be God, and God alone.

THE ORGAN BLOWER

That Mary, the Mother
   Of Jesus may
Have a lovely hymn
   On her festive day,—

That God Almighty
   May be adored
With tuneful treble
   And bass and chord,—

That music may mingle
   With light and flower
On the hot June nights
   At the Holy Hour,—

Humphry, the loon,
   By the dusty rafter,
Sweats like an ox,
   And he says, "I haf ter
Buy new galluses
   The mornin' after!"

ASPIRATION

Perched upon the gable
Above his lonely stable,
(And this is not a fable),

A donkey saw a dove,
With whom he fell in love.
Oh what was he thinking of!

And its soft *tickitacooing*
Almost to his undoing
His wild heart went pursuing.

But a stout rope forefended
What nature never intended,
And his white dream-flight ended.

This poem—breathe no word of it,
Nor bard, nor beast, nor bird of it:—
As though you never heard of it.

THE MILKMAN

When the one o'clock cock begins to crow
  They drag him out of a dream,
And he stares at the stars in the Milky Way
  And the meteors made of cream.

When the sky is a meadow of molten oats
  Sickled with flaming steel,
He hitches his horse to a cart of cans
  With a squeak in its wheezy wheel,

And under the twinkle of sundry suns
  And miscellaneous moons,
His rattling bottles in sleepy lanes
  Tinkle their lonely tunes.

A MUNSTER MEMORY.

All I recall,
(God help us all!)
Is a witless old woman
With shoes and a shawl

Who didn't know when
She had counted to ten
In counting her nine
Baby chicks and a hen

And went crawling behind
In the bushes to find
The little one lost
In a hole in her mind.

NIGHTLY OUTRAGE

They draw the curtains,
  And lock the door;

They keep it dark
  From ten till four

At Small and Small's
  Department Store,

While lackadaisical Elsie
  Scrubs the floor.

Her dress is dirty,
  Her knees are sore,

Pushing her pail
  From ten till four.

I think it's small
  Of Small and Small,

Even though Elsie
  Is lackadaisical,

To pay a woman
  To crawl and crawl

From post to pillar,
  From wall to wall,

And clean their floor
  Like an animal.

I'd rather have
  No floor at all.

NOT EVERY LITTLE MARY

Not every little Mary
  Would come and talk with me,
And whisper me a secret,
  And climb upon my knee;

And ask me, please, to show her
  My silver crucifix,
And say her Pater Noster
  Like good Catholics;

And let me eat a sweet cake,
  And bounce her rubber ball,
And hide me and go-seek me
  Behind the garden wall;

And read me Cinderella
  And the slipper and the fairy.
Some little Marys would,—
  But not every little Mary.

DANNY'S FIRST COMMUNION
(To L. R. S.)

Impotent now the wisdom
   And sword of Solomon
If mothers come to quarrel
   About this little son.

For truly this is Danny,
   And really this is Jesus.
The whole of him is Mary's,
   And all of him Louise's.

SIMPLE SIMONY

When I was short and stumpy
　　And rather golden curled,
For letting a large Archbishop
　　Know Who made the world,

I got a silver dollar
　　So big I couldn't hold it,
So I sat down on a carpet
　　And rolled it, and rolled it.

GRANDMOTHER LOU

Grandmother Lou was a milliner,
  Almost a generation
Ago, but bonnets were still in her
  Imagination,

When, wheeling her out and warming her
  Bones on the sun veranda,
And knowing the trick of charming her,
  Often I'd hand her

A flower or a feather or a twig
  Or a button, or something like that,
Saying: "Wouldn't this ringumadig
  Look nice on a hat?"

And invariably I would wangle
  Into her smile a twinkle,
While along her cheek would dangle
  A ribbony wrinkle;

And a memory gay and bright
  In a faded brain would try
To turn on a delicate light
  In the filmy eye

Of Grandmother Lou, the milliner,
  Who now with the lissome lasses
Of old, lies quiet and still in her
  Grave in the grasses.

And the wind blows over her bonnetless
   Head, and may peace abide her,
Till I shall go rhymeless and sonnetless
   To sleep beside her.

MAGNIFICENCE

Our gentle sister within her mother's heart,
Our tall archangel playing a woman's part,
Still hides a host of childlike fancies whence
Her eyes acquire their stately innocence;
And made two gorgeous wishes and did prevail
At owning a white police-dog and a nightingale.

THE CHILDREN

When I go out walking
  On Bloomsbury Street,
Children say "Here he comes!",
  Children I meet;

The Margarets and Marys
  And Michaels and Mats,
Dropping me curtseys
  And lifting their hats.

The children! The children!
  They load me with love,
In Bloomsbury Gardens
  And Bloomsbury Grove.

By Bloomsbury Chapel
  And Bloomsbury Mart,
I often go walking
  To kindle my heart.

But, when I go out walking
  On Buckingham Lane,
Children say "Here he comes
  Walking again."

The Gladyses, Gwendolyns,
  Grovers and Guys,
Lifting their noses
  And arching their eyes.

The children! The children!
  They hurt me with hate,
In Buckingham Terrace
  And Buckingham Gate.

By Buckingham Mansions
  And Buckingham Inns,
I often go walking
  To pay for my sins.

SARA FINN

Poor old body,
Worn and thin;
Poor old
Sara Finn!

Bent like a snow-bush,
Trudging her own
Way to Eternity
Alone.

No husband,
No family,—
Just Sara,
Just she,

Mumbling "If I'd find
Someone to bury me,
There wouldn't be nothin'
Else to worry me."

Poor Sara, died,
And was buried too.
Peacefully she went,
Spinsters always do;

Like spent candles
When you snuff
Them singly, softly,
Puff! Puff!

Cherubim and Seraphim,
Praise ye the Lord!
Cherubim and Sara Finn,
With one accord!

BETTY'S BIRTHDAY

Angular Annie and buxom Bella
   And tittering Tim were there.
Dick and Dora sat next to Nora,
   And Chubby in Charlie's chair.

Rita and Zita and Paul and Peter,
   Kiddies from A to Zed;
Hiccoughy Humphry and snoozey Susie
   And finnicky Winifred.

The grace was ended, the soup was splendid,
   The chicken was nice and brown.
Papa was present to make it pleasant,
   And mama made us sit down.

She lit three lights on a candle cake
   With nuts and a chocolate border,
And later she cut us a piece apiece
   In all-for-Betty-cal order.

A MATTER FOR CALCULUS

If Millicent Marvel,
  The belle of the town,
Should step from her haughty
  And high estate down

And kiss Rosie Rogers,
  That tired old hag,
Who shines the linoleum
  Wringing a rag:

The tall hats would tumble,
  The lorgnettes would glare;
Some prominent people
  Would swoon on the stair.

If Mortimer Muffins,
  The Mayor of the city,
Should ever, through some
  Preternatural pity,

Embrace Dinny Dooley,
  That battered old man,
Who sweeps in the street
  With a brush and a can:—

The horns would start tooting,
  The traffic would pause
And the length of the block
  Would go wild with guffaws.

Once the astronomers
  Took me apart,
Fixed me a telescope
  Ruled me a chart,

And roundly impressed me
  Revealing how far,
The unthinkable journey
  From star unto star.

But I'm searching for instruments
  Hunting a plan,
That will measure the distance
  From man unto man.

JEREMY

Lucy said to Jeremy, "Jeremy!"
  Jeremy said to Lucy, "What?"
"Don't you remember what day today is?
  Surely you've not forgot?
Didn't you notice the special pudding,
  And the little blue vase of flowers?
Whose anniversary is it, Jeremy?"
  Jeremy said to Lucy, "Ours."

Lucy said to Jeremy, "Jeremy!"
  Jeremy said to Lucy, "What?"
"I've been waiting till I've been weary
  Keeping your supper hot.
All day long I've been so excited!
  Didn't you like your tea?
How many years are we married, Jeremy?"
  Jeremy said to Lucy, "Three."

Lucy said to Jeremy, "Jeremy!"
  Jeremy said to Lucy, "What?"
"You seem dreadfully unromantic;
  Maybe we fuss a lot,
But aren't we still the same old lovers,
  Summer and winter through?
Tell me who was your sweetheart, Jeremy?"
  Jeremy said to Lucy, "You."

Lucy said to Jeremy, "Jeremy!"
  Jeremy said to Lucy, "What?"
"Remember the first year we were married,
  Out in the garden plot?

The moon was lovely, and you said I had
　　Something as blue as skies.
What did I have so pretty, Jeremy?"
　　Jeremy said to Lucy, "Eyes."

Lucy said to Jeremy, "Jeremy!"
　　Jeremy said to Lucy, "What?"
"Remember the winter we went to dances?
　　Remember the gown I bought?
We danced one night at the Grand Pavilion,
　　And you wore an evening suit;
And how did you say your wife looked, Jeremy?"
　　Jeremy said to Lucy, "Cute."

Lucy said to Jeremy, "Jeremy!"
　　Jeremy said to Lucy, "What?"
"Remember the time when we had birthdays,
　　And wasn't it nice you thought
To buy me bows for my satin slippers,
　　Because I had tiny feet!
And what did you have to call them, Jeremy?"
　　Jeremy said to Lucy, "Sweet."

Lucy said to Jeremy, "Jeremy!"
　　Jeremy said to Lucy, "What?"
"Remember the poems we read together,
　　The Maiden of Camelot
And the Knight who lived in a wondrous castle,
　　Holding her hand in his?
Didn't they used to thrill us, Jeremy?"
　　Jeremy said to Lucy, "Zzzzzz!"

THE LITTLE RED ROSARY

Old Annie's little red rosary
  Old Annie loved the best,
Her little red chain of cherry stones
  The priest had blessed.

"Hail Mary . . . full of grace . . ."
  Over and over again.
Even after she fell asleep
  And the clock struck ten,

Old Annie's thumb and finger
  Would fumble along alone
And hunt for the next Hail Mary
  On the next cherry stone

With no Old Annie to guide them.
  And after her prayer had stopped,
It would be nearly a minute
  Till the little red rosary dropped.

THE MARRIAGE MAKERS

Today I married Martha,
  I married her to Jim.
He was huge and handsome,
  She was sweet and slim.

We went to make a wedding,
  Boy, girl, and priest,
Before Our Lady's altar,
  Upon Our Lady's feast.

She in her dove-white slippers
  Stood on the marble stair;
He was a faultless bridegroom,
  Beaming from heels to hair.

And linking their lives together,
  Getting their story told,
I too was rather splendid,
  Vested in gown of gold.

Lifting her lily finger,
  Looped in a yellow band,
I helped him to tell the message
  Her heart would understand.

We managed it all in whispers,
  And mine were the phrases lent
To Love in its perfect moment,
  Love in its Sacrament.

But now when the Mass is over
  And off they ride to town,
Alone by Our Lady's altar
  I wait in my golden gown,

Robed in my shining armor,
  Girded for God to guess
How in my white betrothal,
  All in my loneliness

Merry I make espousals,
  Hiding no secret sorrow:—
And I shall marry Rosemary
  And Christopher tomorrow.

NICE SURPRISE

Eileen has got a new baby boy,
  We call him our "nice surprise",
With genuine fingers, authentic toes,
  And actual ears and eyes;

Able to gurgle and breathe and smile,
  Able to coo and sing,
Roly and poly and sweet and small
  And pretty as anything.

He knows we can hardly believe he's real,
  He knows he's nice and new;
But minute by minute and hour by hour
  He keeps on being true.

MRS. WHITTLE

I'm 'bout
Worn out . . .

I'm nearly
Eighty three

You know,
And so

I guess I'm
Near my time . . .

I gits
Coughin' fits

Terrible,
I'll tell

You
I do . . .

But that ain't
My worst complaint . . .

I sleep light
At night . . .

My heart
'll start

Pumpin'
An' thumpin'

'N I wakes
With headaches . . .

My stomach
Has gone back

On me
Awfully;

I gits sick
'N anemic.

Guess my blood
Ain't good . . .

Sally's dead.
So's Ed . . .

These
Were my babies . . .

John,
He's gone . . .

He was my husband
And

I ain't got
No one but

Jeff,
'N he's deaf,

'N Mame,
An' she's lame . . .

They're weary
Tendin' me,

Fetchin' my cushion
'N pushin'

My wheel-chair
Everywhere . . .

They're fed
Up, they said . . .

They say I'm
All the time

In the way.
That's what they say . . .

So don't show 'em
This *poem*.

BESSIE

You may be Polly the pretty,
You may be Winnie the witty,
You may be showy and I may be shy,—
My plainness I do not deny;
But let me be Bessie the baker,
The jelly-roll maker,
Give me a flour to my fancy,
I'll please your palate and eye.

You may be Charlotte the charming,
You may be Anne the alarming,
I may be stupid and you may be spry,—
But doughnuts are something to fry;
Let me be Bessie the baker,
The cookie-prize taker,
Someone will need me and know me,
Someone will come bye and bye.

You may have beautiful tresses
And trinkets and diamonds and dresses,
But do your hot blueberry muffins
Evoke exclamations like "My!"?
Let me be Bessie the baker,
The appetite waker,
Hiding my heart in a dumpling,
Wooing my prince with a pie.

OBSEQUIES IN EBONY

The black folk up in Harlem
　　Are simple in belief,
Are lightsome in their laughter,
　　But gorgeous in their grief.

They make of death a festival
　　As Christians ought, in brief,
They make death so magnificent
　　It gave my soul relief:—

When crowds of dusky damsels
　　Came flocking out of flats,
In deep memorial muslins
　　And swanky Sunday hats;

And droves of dapper darkies
　　With canes and cravats,
In wonderful waistcoats
　　And spectacular spats,

Carried a costly coffin,
　　And boomed the biggest bell,
And horrified a heretic
　　And shocked an infidel,

Assisting at the Service
　　Which I chanted extra well,
With special robes and rubrics
　　For a Roman Catholic swell.

NOEL

When I said Mass at midnight
  And candles were aglow
I saw a white old woman
  Two thousand years ago,

My very great grandmother
  Who spun me flesh and bone,
Who felt my fingers aching
  In the atoms of her own,

In whom my eyes were shining
  However far away,
When Christ was in His cradle
  And it was Christmas Day.

WIND REQUIEM

Josephine, Josephine, gaily go.
Your White Lover is whispering, the moon is low;
Down through the sky wastes a broken star is falling;
Be up, maid, and hurrying, and hear how tenderly He
  is calling.

Run soft as you can, wake no one; be a little mouse on
  the stair.
Wrap as you run a ribbon around your wind-
  scampering hair.
Slim, slender and pale, slip out through the narrow
  gate,
Josephine, and by the wheely waters of the lonely mill
  wait.

An owl or two owls will hoot in the hedge, maybe, and
  a chattering squirrel will run;
Be unafraid of any noises, though there may be many
  noises, but listen carefully for one:
His Voice in the dark, alone in the wood, by the moon-
  wavering water,
Soft halooing "Are you there? Are you coming home
  to Heaven, Josephine, my daughter?"

TO A YOUNG POET

When lightly cracks the eager egg
   That holds the ripening bluebird,
Nor can contain within its shell
   The knocking of a new bird:—

He reels and rushes with delight
   Melodiously abroad
To fill at noon the sunny lull
   Between the cloud and the clod,

Where flew at night the ancient owl
   Who croaked a flimsy tune,
And spoiled the lovely stillnesses
   Between the mole and the moon.

FAREWELL TO OXFORD

Long is the road that leads me to the high
White altitudes where I can ululate
My ultimate, un-get-at-able good bye,
(Hooking the little hook behind the gate).
God knows where I shall now eventuate
(A darlin' word), in what United State
I'll groan a grief and sibilate a sigh.

This parenthetical, provoking whine
Sounds like a dose of Browning, doesn't it?
But blubbering in brackets is so fine
For keeping sentiment indefinite.
(So let me bracket up this little bit
For sake of what's forsaken), when I quit
Eric and Nigel, Anne and Caroline.

All must be symbols, all must be undersaid.
This is the rule that keeps the game sublime.
Our goal is cloudwards and a golden thread
Falls down a mountain that is steep to climb.
But when our spirits scale the heights they dread
And lose aloofness like a load of lead,
Some meaning may be made of, light be shed
Upon this ruthless and ungraceful rhyme.

THE FROST

The frost has come. I feel a nip
On lid and lobe and lock and lip.

It won't be long until the day
It eats my head and heart away.

TO OUR BLESSED LORD AT THE PILLAR

On Thee, Whom jibe and threatening could not press
    To flinch at a flogging for my guiltiness,
I pray that my lash, not the least to fall,
    At least may not fall heaviest of all.

EPILOGUE

My name was written in Thy cup
That I should one day lift it up,
   My heart and head above.
This be my art, my only gift,
To learn to love the cup I lift,
   And lift the cup I love,
Carolling in between the times
Some tuneful riddles and little rhymes.